A poem occasioned by a view of Powers-court House, the improvements, park, &c. Inscribed to Richard Wingfield, Esq.

A poem occasioned by a view of Powers-court House, the improvements, park, &c. Inscribed to Richard Wingfield, Esq.

Multiple Contributors, See Notes
ESTCID: T089358
Reproduction from British Library
Variously attributed to Walter Chamberlain and to John Towers.
Dublin : printed by George Faulkner, 1741.
[2],13,[1]p. ; 8°

Eighteenth Century
Collections Online
Print Editions

Gale ECCO Print Editions

Relive history with *Eighteenth Century Collections Online*, now available in print for the independent historian and collector. This series includes the most significant English-language and foreign-language works printed in Great Britain during the eighteenth century, and is organized in seven different subject areas including literature and language; medicine, science, and technology; and religion and philosophy. The collection also includes thousands of important works from the Americas.

The eighteenth century has been called "The Age of Enlightenment." It was a period of rapid advance in print culture and publishing, in world exploration, and in the rapid growth of science and technology – all of which had a profound impact on the political and cultural landscape. At the end of the century the American Revolution, French Revolution and Industrial Revolution, perhaps three of the most significant events in modern history, set in motion developments that eventually dominated world political, economic, and social life.

In a groundbreaking effort, Gale initiated a revolution of its own: digitization of epic proportions to preserve these invaluable works in the largest online archive of its kind. Contributions from major world libraries constitute over 175,000 original printed works. Scanned images of the actual pages, rather than transcriptions, recreate the works *as they first appeared.*

Now for the first time, these high-quality digital scans of original works are available via print-on-demand, making them readily accessible to libraries, students, independent scholars, and readers of all ages.

For our initial release we have created seven robust collections to form one the world's most comprehensive catalogs of 18th century works.

Initial Gale ECCO Print Editions collections include:

History and Geography

Rich in titles on English life and social history, this collection spans the world as it was known to eighteenth-century historians and explorers. Titles include a wealth of travel accounts and diaries, histories of nations from throughout the world, and maps and charts of a world that was still being discovered. Students of the War of American Independence will find fascinating accounts from the British side of conflict.

Social Science

Delve into what it was like to live during the eighteenth century by reading the first-hand accounts of everyday people, including city dwellers and farmers, businessmen and bankers, artisans and merchants, artists and their patrons, politicians and their constituents. Original texts make the American, French, and Industrial revolutions vividly contemporary.

Medicine, Science and Technology

Medical theory and practice of the 1700s developed rapidly, as is evidenced by the extensive collection, which includes descriptions of diseases, their conditions, and treatments. Books on science and technology, agriculture, military technology, natural philosophy, even cookbooks, are all contained here.

Literature and Language

Western literary study flows out of eighteenth-century works by Alexander Pope, Daniel Defoe, Henry Fielding, Frances Burney, Denis Diderot, Johann Gottfried Herder, Johann Wolfgang von Goethe, and others. Experience the birth of the modern novel, or compare the development of language using dictionaries and grammar discourses.

Religion and Philosophy

The Age of Enlightenment profoundly enriched religious and philosophical understanding and continues to influence present-day thinking. Works collected here include masterpieces by David Hume, Immanuel Kant, and Jean-Jacques Rousseau, as well as religious sermons and moral debates on the issues of the day, such as the slave trade. The Age of Reason saw conflict between Protestantism and Catholicism transformed into one between faith and logic -- a debate that continues in the twenty-first century.

Law and Reference

This collection reveals the history of English common law and Empire law in a vastly changing world of British expansion. Dominating the legal field is the *Commentaries of the Law of England* by Sir William Blackstone, which first appeared in 1765. Reference works such as almanacs and catalogues continue to educate us by revealing the day-to-day workings of society.

Fine Arts

The eighteenth-century fascination with Greek and Roman antiquity followed the systematic excavation of the ruins at Pompeii and Herculaneum in southern Italy; and after 1750 a neoclassical style dominated all artistic fields. The titles here trace developments in mostly English-language works on painting, sculpture, architecture, music, theater, and other disciplines. Instructional works on musical instruments, catalogs of art objects, comic operas, and more are also included.

The BiblioLife Network

This project was made possible in part by the BiblioLife Network (BLN), a project aimed at addressing some of the huge challenges facing book preservationists around the world. The BLN includes libraries, library networks, archives, subject matter experts, online communities and library service providers. We believe every book ever published should be available as a high-quality print reproduction; printed on-demand anywhere in the world. This insures the ongoing accessibility of the content and helps generate sustainable revenue for the libraries and organizations that work to preserve these important materials.

The following book is in the "public domain" and represents an authentic reproduction of the text as printed by the original publisher. While we have attempted to accurately maintain the integrity of the original work, there are sometimes problems with the original work or the micro-film from which the books were digitized. This can result in minor errors in reproduction. Possible imperfections include missing and blurred pages, poor pictures, markings and other reproduction issues beyond our control. Because this work is culturally important, we have made it available as part of our commitment to protecting, preserving, and promoting the world's literature.

GUIDE TO FOLD-OUTS MAPS and OVERSIZED IMAGES

The book you are reading was digitized from microfilm captured over the past thirty to forty years. Years after the creation of the original microfilm, the book was converted to digital files and made available in an online database.

In an online database, page images do not need to conform to the size restrictions found in a printed book. When converting these images back into a printed bound book, the page sizes are standardized in ways that maintain the detail of the original. For large images, such as fold-out maps, the original page image is split into two or more pages

Guidelines used to determine how to split the page image follows:

• Some images are split vertically; large images require vertical and horizontal splits.
• For horizontal splits, the content is split left to right.
• For vertical splits, the content is split from top to bottom.
• For both vertical and horizontal splits, the image is processed from top left to bottom right.

A

P O E M

OCCASIONED

By a VIEW of

Powers-court Houſe,

THE

Improvements, Park, &c.

Inſcribed to

RICHARD WINGFIELD, Eſq;

Dii tibi divitias dederant, artemq; fruendi.   Hor.

D U B L I N:
Printed by GEORGE FAULKNER, in *Eſſex-Street,*
MDCCXLI.

A

P O E M

Occafioned by a View of

Powers-court Houfe,

THE Mufe forgetting, by the Mufe forgot,

And what I relifh leaft, become my Lot,

Doom'd to a Country Church remote and poor,

And what is ftill more dreadful, ferve the Cure——

No Sprig of Laurel left, but in my Pews,

How can I write? yet how fhall I refufe?

A   My

My Life, a loitring fedentary Calm!

My Tafte for Song——a penitential Pfalm!

Much tir'd I am, with hearing News from *Spain*,

And quite perplex'd concerning *Carthagene*,   10

What Method then to pleafe fhall I purfue?

For once I'll venture——and indite to you.

To me, you cry! pray Sir on what Pretence?

——A juft Efteem for Candour, and good Senfe,

For the plain Heart, benevolent Defign,   15

The Warmth Humane, or if you will, Divine.

What Name becomes you beft? one late in Print,

——The *Man of Rofs*, feems no improper Hint,

Whofe gracious Gates, like yours, receiv'd the Poor,

Nay, more your Merit—for your Fortune's more!

Like his, your Worth fincere and not a Sound,

Like him a Blefling——to your Country round,

To

To him Age, Want, and Sickneſs paid their Vow,

That Man thus thought, and liv'd—as you do now.

Charm'd with this Theme, tho' indolent ſo long,

With Proſe bemus'd, quite reprobate in Song,

In Awe I reaſſume the votive Pen,

And (Peace be to *Apollo)* write again.

Me, *Cynthius* check'd in early Life's Career,

Deſiſt he cry'd, and gently tipp'd my Ear, 30

Deſiſt from Verſe, an Art beyond your Reach,

But (tho' a Heathen God) he bid me Preach:

I bow'd, aſſented, and ſubmiſſive choſe,

To abdicate the Lyre, and drudge in Proſe.

But ſhould Fate lead me to a Work like thine, 35

My Boſom kindles, and my Thoughts refine,

With ſofteſt Verſe I preſs the Muſe once more,

And (not to break old Cuſtoms) thus implore,

Attend in Sky-dipt Robes, ye fmiling *Hours,*   40

Unlock your Cryftal Springs, and Moffy Bowers,

Crowd each luxuriant Image Wit can feign,

And paint, O Mufe, the Eye-enchanting Scene,

Give Wings to Thought, to rapid Fancy Fire—

—The meaneft Judge can gaze, and juft admire. 45

Romantick Region ! where I turn my Eyes

Elyzian-walks, and claffick Landfkips rife !

Enthufiaftic Fancy feems to fee

A *Tempe* bloom, for fuch fhall *Pow'rs-court* be.

O let, my rapt Imagination trace,   50

The Site, and Sylvan Genius of the Place,

Where Nature varies, yet unites each Part,

And Chance reflects Advantages to Art;

Or let my Eyes in bold Excurfions gain,

The fwelling *Vifta,* and the finking Plain,   55

Where

(Where a free Heav'n the Sight's wide Empire fills,

Then melts in diftant Clouds, and blueifh Hills.)

Or gently catch'd by Views more regular

Take in the verdant Slope, and rais'd Parterre.

Hence, from this *Tafte*, are Numbers pleas'd and

  fed,   60

The Wife have Pleafure, the Diftrefs'd have Bread,

This Tafte brings Profit, and improves with Senfe,

And through a thoufand Channels turns Expence,

Benevolence in num'rous Streams imparts,

And ends in Virtue what began in Arts,   65

Removes fharp Famine, Sicknefs, and Defpair,

Relieves the afking Eye, the rifing Tear,

Such Woe, as late o'er pale *Hibernia* paft,

—And fuch (ye Guardian Powers) we wifh the laft.

If publick Spirit fhines, 'tis juft at leaft   70

To give fome Glory too, to *publick Tafte*,

     A 3 .   Which

Which bids proud Art the pillar'd Fabrick raife,

Scoops the rough Rock, and levels vaft High-ways

Plans future Woods, for Profpect and Defence,

And forms a Bower a hundred Summers hence, 75

Ideal Groves, and Beautys juft in View ———

But fuch (my Friend) as Time fhall bring to you,

Frefh blow your Gardens! intermingl'd Scene!

Soft Carpet Walks, and Green encircling Green,

A chequer'd Space, alternate Sun, and Shade,

The Country round, one wide delicious Glade!

Enamel'd Vales with fair Horizons bound, 80

Here tow'ring Woods, and pendant Rock-work

　　　round!

With graceful Sweeps here mazy Windings run,

Or gently meet in Lines where they begun,

Here gufhes down fteep Steps a ductile Rill,

There fpreads in fluid Azure, broad, and ftill, 85

So

So mix'd the Views, so exquisitely shewn,

Each flow'ry Field, and Valley seems your own,

While Nature smiles, obsequious to your Call,

Directs, assists, and recommends it all.

At last she gives (O Art how vain thy Aid)   90

To crown the beauteous Work, a vast Cascade.

Say Muse, who listens where the *Shannon* roars,

Which once divided Empires with its Shoars,

Tell in her western Course immense, and fair,

Can all the Falls and Cataracts compare?

Let grand *Versailles* her liquid Landskips boast,

Pure Scenes of Nature here, delight us most,

Her rudest Prospects bid the Fancy start,

And snatch the Soul beyond the Works of Art——

O would some Master Hand, adorn thy Walls, 100

And catch the living Fountain as it falls,

The

The gay Original would crown thy Dome,

—And you then boaſt your nobleſt Scene at Home.

Lo! down the Rock which Clouds and Darkneſs

   hide

In wild Mæanders Spouts a Silver Tide ;   104

Or ſprung from dropping Miſts or wintry Rills,

Rolls the large Tribute of the Cloud-topp'd Hills ;

But ſhou'd the damp-wing'd Tempeſt keenly blow

With whiſtling Torrents, and deſcending Snow,

In one huge Heap the ſhow'ry Whirlpools ſwell,

And deluge wide the Tract where firſt they fell 111

'Til from the headlong Verge of yon black Steep,

A tumbling River; roars intenſe and deep.

From Rock to Rock its boiling Stream is broke,

And all below, the Waters fall in Smoak—— 115

So vaſt the Height no Diſtance ſeems between

The Mountain Summit, and the blue *Serene*,

So wond'rous high the floping Torrents roll,

Such ftill Amazement fixes all the Soul!

So hoarfe the Thunder of the rufhing Tide!　　120

The Ears can fcarce receive a Sound befide.

Tho' the green Glades with one wild Concert ring,

And up the Woodland warbles all the Spring.———

Juft where the Beam of Sight diftended fails,　　125

Up the clear *Infinite* the Eagle fails;

Or half Way down the Precipice's Head,

White ling'ring Fogs, and dew-bright Clouds are
　　　　fpread,

The Soul from Indolence to Rapture wakes,

'Till on th' unfolding Ear the Water breaks,

This Sound when Night has fadden'd all the Skyes,

The Traveller hears far with wild Surprize:

High o'er the waving Landfkip dark with Trees,

A diftant Murmur fwells upon the Breeze:

Now

Now near, now dying varies with each Blaft

Then fettles in a fullen Roar at laft.   135

Thus, where the *Nile*'s firft parent Urn is found

Her Catara&ts rufh down, (a dizzy Sound)

Wide and more wide, the dreadful Ecchoes run

Beyond the burning Zone, and meet the Sun.

Defcription flags——let Thought the reft exprefs

A Theme untouch'd, delicious to Excefs,

Profufe of all the Soul can wifh or love,

—A Landfkip in the Golden Dreams of *Jove!*

O that my Breaft with *Pæan*'s Flame were fmit,

Or ardent as my Wifh, fublime my Wit :   145

(If for a Verfe like mine I cou'd engage)

This deathlefs Stream fhou'd murmur through an

    Age.

But ftop fond Mufe, or foar to bolder Lays,

The finifh'd Seat demands the Founder's Praife,

                            Where

Where Taste sets off, and dignifies Expence,

Neat without Glare, Magnificent with Sense;

As in some Piece a *Titian*'s Hand has wrought,

The fair Result, and Eloquence of Thought;

Where Light and Shadow blend in social Strife

And ev'ry glorious Colour streams with Life; 145

Thus, in Improvements shines the *Attick* Taste,

Thus *Eden* springs where once you found a Waste.

Sketch'd in your House the candid Heart we view,

Its Grace, Strength, Order, all reflecting you.

Yet pleas'd to see, and fonder still to tell, 160

Your candid Heart becomes that House so well;

The mirthful Look, kind Air, without Controul,

The easy Converse, and the Flow of Soul.

How flush'd my Thought! how pleas'd my Eye survey'd,

The gilt *Profil*, and pictur'd *Colonnade*! 165

There

There arch'd *Hesperian* Windows drink the Noon,

Here fluted *Dorics* rear the rich *Saloon*,

The Pile all round for gazing Homage calls,

In Fretwork Cielings and hiftoric Walls,

Ætherial Dyes the glowing Canvas ftain,   170

Where *Italy* prefents a Summer-fcene;

Now beats my Heart, or emulous I burn,

At *Tully*'s Tufculum, or *Virgil*'s Urn,

Still green with Bays the hallow'd Ruins ftand,

Still crown'd with Fame the hallow'd Names com-

        mand;

Full on my confcious Soul their Glories ftrike,

And for your Sake I figh to write unlike———

But for thefe Rhimes (yet menacing fome more)

Mean as thefe are, their Paffage I implore,

I know your Judgment polifh'd, yet Humane, 180

Your Temper apt to give that Judgment Pain,

                                    Difpos'd

Difpos'd to Think, to feel for humane Race,

And ftill in this bad Age to fhew fome Grace ;

To act as Reafon and good Senfe infpire,

——Ah how unlike the modern Country Squire!

By your Applaufe Verfe (low as mine) can live,

Nor can I make more Faults, than you forgive.

F I N I S.

Lightning Source UK Ltd.
Milton Keynes UK
UKHW050819100622
404239UK00006B/367